A Finding-Out Book

THE FARM

By Solveig Paulson Russell

Illustrated by Shelley Fink

Parents' Magazine Press • New York

Text Copyright © 1970 by Solveig Paulson Russell
Illustrations Copyright © 1970 by Parents' Magazine Press
All rights reserved
Printed in the United States of America
International Standard Book Number: 0-8193-0363-1
Library of Congress Catalog Card Number: 76-87740
10 9 8 7 6 5 4 3 2

Contents

Planting	6
Watering	11
Spraying	14
Harvesting	15
What Plants Grow on the Farm?	19
Machines	24
Spring, Summer, Fall, and Winter	26
Animals on the Farm	30
Buildings on the Farm	39
How Does the Farmer's Wife Help on the Farm?	46
How Do the Children Help?	49
How Does the Farm Family Have Fun Together?	52
How Does the Farmer Make the Best Use of His Land?	56
How Has Farm Life Changed?	58
Index	62

Most of the people in our country do not live on farms. But those who do are very important. Without farmers we could not live. The work farmers do gives us food and clothing.

Farmers work hard. They raise different kinds of things—plants and animals. Whatever is raised is called a crop. Many farmers raise only one or two kinds of crops. When a farm has only one or two crops it is a *specialized* farm. A *general* farm is one on which more than one or two crops are raised. Long ago all farms were general farms. Now there are a great many specialized farms. But there are still general farms, too.

Planting

The first work a farmer must do to grow any kind of a plant crop is to get the ground ready. Plants need ground that is fine and loose. The farmer breaks up hard ground by plowing it. Plows are heavy machines with strong blades that cut through the ground. They lift it up and turn it over in long rows, or furrows. Plows, and other machines, are now usually pulled by tractors. But long ago horses, mules, and even oxen, pulled the plows.

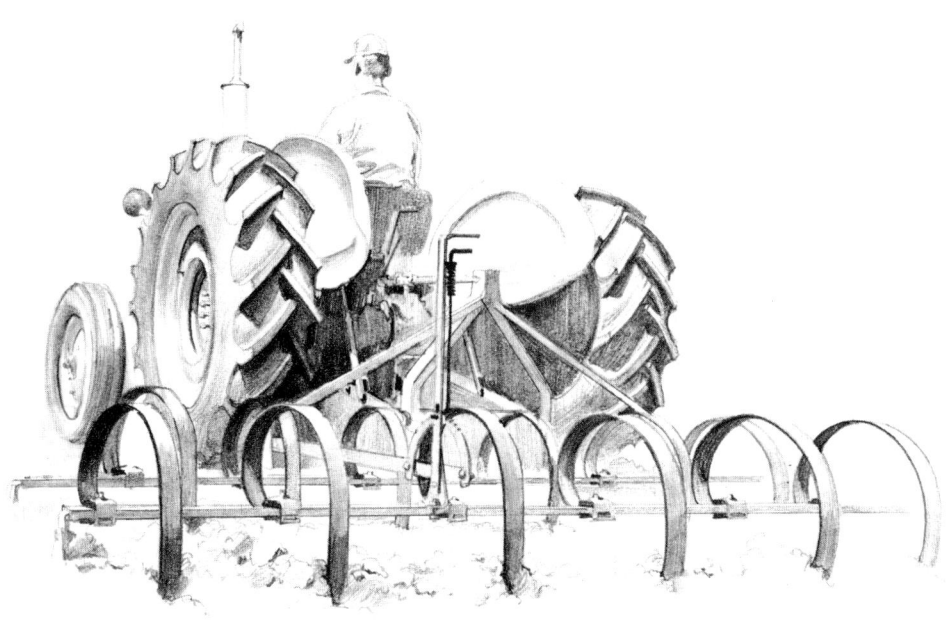

The ground is broken up by plowing. But plowing does not make the ground fine enough for planting. Many big lumps of dirt are left after plowing. The farmer breaks up these lumps with a machine called a *cultivator*.

Cultivators used after plowing are either harrows or disks. Harrows have strong metal teeth, straight or curved. The teeth are set in a heavy metal frame. When a harrow is pulled, its teeth comb through the ground.

A disk has a row of sharp round metal parts that look like solid wheels. They are set close together on a frame. These turn as the disk is pulled. Disks cut the ground, making it fine.

Farmers use disks when they want to cut deeply into the ground. A harrow does not stir the ground as deeply as a disk does. Some kinds of ground need disking, other kinds need harrowing after being plowed.

Before farmers had cultivators, they had to chop the ground with hand hoes to break it up.

When the land has been made ready, the farmer plants his seed. If he is going to raise a grain crop he uses a grain seeder. Wheat, oats, barley, and rye are grains. The grain seeder is a machine that holds seeds in big boxes. It has little pipes that let the seeds drop evenly to the ground. Often a harrow is hooked behind the seeder. The harrow covers the seeds with soil so they can grow.

When farmers plant crops that grow in rows, they use row seeders. These work like grain seeders. But they leave spaces between the rows of seed. Sugar beets, cotton, corn, and many vegetables are row crops.

Some row crops, such as strawberries, must be planted by hand. These crops are started with small plants taken from larger plants. The small plants are called cuttings, or runners. When a farmer plants these, he has to bend over and set each one into the ground. This kind of planting is very hard work.

Watering

As crops grow, a farmer must water, or irrigate, those that need watering. In some parts of the country there is plenty of rain. Then the farmer does not have to water his crops. Grain crops usually get enough water from rain.

Some farmers are lucky enough to have streams nearby. They dig ditches from the streams to their fields. Then the water can run through the ditches to water the crops.

Sometimes farmers use pipes and sprinklers for watering. The water for these comes from a stream or a well with a machine pump. Most farmers dig wells for water. They make a well by digging or drilling a deep hole until they reach underground water, just as you may sometimes have reached water when you dug in sand. The water from rain and snow soaks into the ground all year. It forms pools or streams deep in the ground. Farmers use electricity to pump the water from wells to their houses and fields.

In some parts of our country farmers use windmills for irrigating or for watering animals. These are tall metal towers. At the top there is a circle with four large arms, or blades, or a circle with many smaller blades.

A child's pinwheel is a kind of windmill. When the wind blows against a pinwheel it turns. When winds blow against a windmill's blades they turn. As the windmill turns, it makes machines on the windmill move. The machines are fastened to water pumps. When a windmill turns, its machine pumps water from the ground.

Spraying

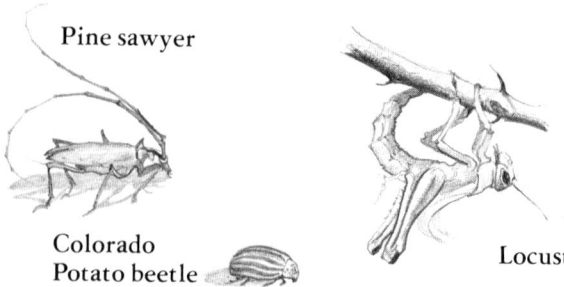

Some insects are harmful to plants. The farmer kills them by using insect spray on his crops. He often has to do this a number of times. There are many kinds of spraying machines. All of them make a fine mist of spray that settles on the plants. The spray kills the insects as they eat the crops.

On very large farms airplanes are used for spraying. They sweep over the fields. As they fly, a fine spray drops down from them, covering the plants.

Spray is poison, so people who use it must be very careful with it. Those who use spraying machines wear masks so they won't breathe the spray. They have clothes used only for spraying.

Harvesting

Harvesting time is the time when the crops are gathered. It is a busy time for the farmer, but usually a happy one. It is a happy time because a good harvest means that all the farmer's hard work has given him good crops.

Grain is harvested by machines called combines that cut and thresh it at the same time. Threshing is separating the grain heads from the plant stalks. Combines are big machines that have their own engines to pull them, just as automobiles do.

Long ago all grain harvesting was done by hand. Farmers had to cut grain with long curved knives. They had to tie it into bundles. Then they beat it with sticks, or made heavy animals walk on it to get the grain threshed.

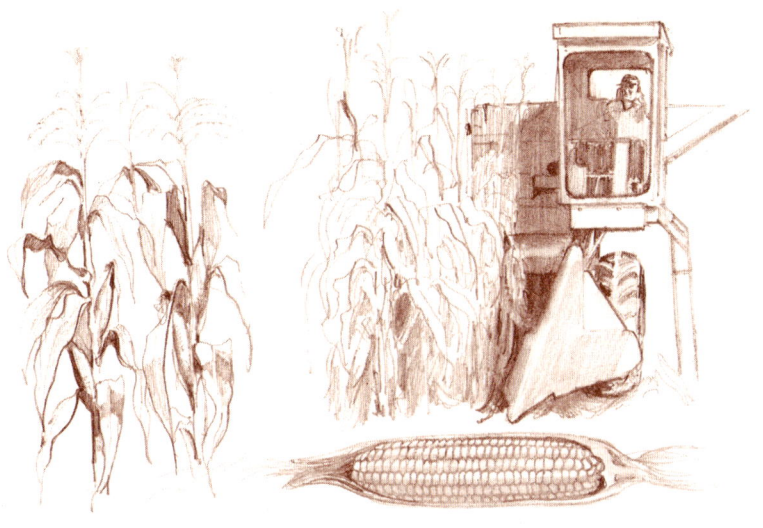

Corn stalks may be cut by machines while the plants and corn ears are green. They are chopped up to be fed to animals in winter. But corn to be used as grain is left to grow until the ears are ripe. The kernels on ripe corn ears are yellow and hard. A corn-harvesting combine strips the ears from the plants and takes the kernels from the cobs. The corn grain is then stored in bins. Corn makes good food for both animals and people.

Long ago people picked and shelled the corn ears by hand. Or they fed the whole ears to animals and let them eat the corn kernels from the cobs. Now farms where much corn is raised use machines for harvesting it.

Farmers who raise fruit and vegetables must know just when to harvest them. If fruit is to go a long way to market it cannot be so ripe that it will be bruised or spoiled by the time it is used. For this reason fruit for markets is usually picked before it is really ripe. Then it can travel without being hurt and have time to ripen more before use. But if fruit is to be used by the farmer's family or neighbors it can be picked when it is sweet and ready to eat.

Most vegetables travel better than most fruit. But they, too, must be picked so they will reach markets in good shape.

Fruits and vegetables are usually picked by hand. Machines are used on some big specialized farms.

What Plants Grow on the Farm?

Grain, vegetables, and fruits are found on most farms. All of them are food for animals and people.

Grain can be fed to animals just as it is harvested. But before people use them grains are usually made into flour or breakfast cereal. Bread, macaroni, and cereals all come from grain.

Tomatoes, beans, potatoes, beets, lettuce, carrots, and onions are field and garden vegetables. Can you think of any others? Vegetables are good for people and for some animals such as pigs and rabbits.

Farms that raise vegetables for city people to eat fresh are called truck farms. Truck farms are usually close to big cities. Each day hundreds of loads of fresh vegetables are brought to stores on the farmers' trucks. Without the truck farmers people in cities would not eat well. And without city people who eat fresh vegetables, the truck farmers would have no work.

There are many kinds of fruit. Apples, pears, peaches, cherries, oranges, grapefruit, and berries are a few kinds. You will be able to think of other kinds that you like. Most fruit is raised on specialized farms. But many general farms have some fruit to use and sell also.

Like vegetables, fruit is sold fresh in markets. But a large part of both fruit and vegetable crops is sent to factories to be canned or frozen.

In warm parts of our country farmers grow cotton, rice, tobacco, sugar cane, and peanuts.

Specialized farms raise flowers and plants. They are sold to florists and to families for home gardens, or yards, or window boxes. A farm that raises plants and flowers to sell is called a nursery. Most nurseries have glass buildings, called hothouses or greenhouses. The hothouses protect the plants from cold but let them get plenty of light, so they can be grown all through the year.

Some farms raise only trees. Some of these are Christmas tree farms. Others are large forests where trees are grown for their wood. The wood is used for buildings, furniture, and firewood. Some tree farms raise only nut trees.

Machines

Machines are important for farm work, and farmers take good care of them. They usually have one or two trucks and tractors. They may have other special machines besides those we have already talked about. These could be mowers, rakes, ditch diggers, and such other machines as special crop pickers.

Farmers use their trucks to carry crops when the crops are ready to be sold. The farmers sometimes take the crops to towns to be sold in stores. Most fruits and vegetables go to canneries to be canned. Or they go to freezing plants to be frozen. Grain crops are often taken to railroad cars. The cars take the grain to different factories where it is made into flour, breakfast food, and other food for people and animals.

Spring, Summer, Fall, and Winter

Each season has special tasks for farmers. In spring they plant seeds in fields and gardens to get crops started. They care for the baby animals born then. They spray trees and other plants to kill insects.

Only a small part of our country has sugar maple trees. But if sugar maple trees grow on a farm their owners make syrup. Men gather the tree sap in early spring. Then they boil the sap until it becomes syrup. When the first settlers came to our country the Indians taught them how to make maple syrup.

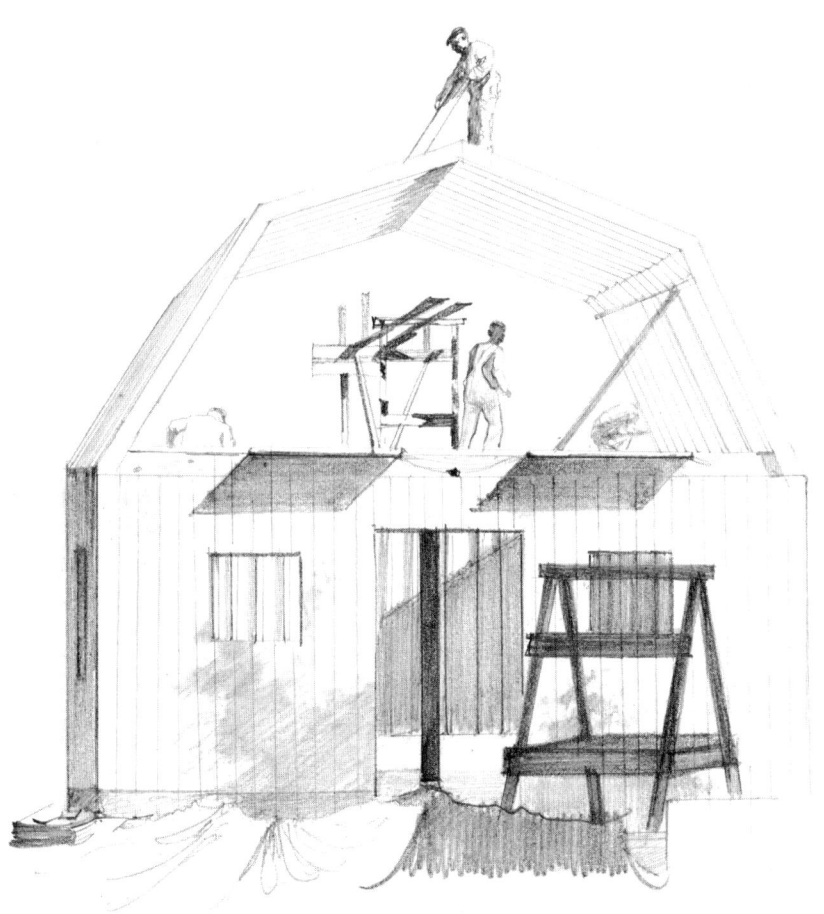

In summer farmers cut hay and take it to the barns. It is used for feeding cattle. They harvest some fruits and vegetables and take them to market. If they have cows, they cut and chop green corn to feed to the cows in the winter. They irrigate crops that need water. They paint the outside of buildings, and build new ones.

Fall brings the harvesting of grain and other crops. In fall farmers get ready for colder days. They make sure they have enough food for their animals. On farms where wood is still burned for heat, farmers cut down trees and saw them up for wood.

Winter gives farmers a chance to take care of the inside of buildings and to work on their machines. Machines all need oil on their moving parts. They need paint so they will not get rusty. Farmers must see to it that their machines are always ready for use. They are careful in using them, and watchful for everyone's safety. Farm children are taught to stay away from farm machines.

In winter animals need special care. And winter is a good time for farmers to plan for the next year.

Animals on the Farm

Cows are female cattle. Bulls are male cattle. Calves are baby cattle. Calves drink milk from their mothers. Cattle are important farm animals because they are very useful to people. From the skin, or hide, of cows and bulls, people make leather. Cattle hoofs can be made into glue. Horns can be made into buttons. The meat from grown cattle is called beef. Calf meat is veal.

Some cattle are raised for beef, and some for milk. The farms where beef cattle are raised are called cattle ranches.

Many general farms keep a cow or two to give the family milk. Some farms raise nothing but milk cows. These are dairy farms. Dairy farms sell milk for drinking and for making butter and cheese.

Horses used to be very important farm animals before farmers had tractors. Now very few horses are used for pulling loads. General farms may keep a horse or two to help with light work. But mostly they are pets for children to ride. On cattle ranches in the West cowboys still use horses to round up cattle.

Baby horses are called foals. They drink milk from their mothers until they are old enough to eat grass.

Many farms raise pigs for their meat. We call the meat pork, and ham, and bacon. Pig fat makes lard. Pig skin is used for some kinds of leather. Footballs, purses, and gloves are often made from pigskin. The tough hair from pigs is used for making brushes.

Little pigs drink milk from their mothers.

Pigs are sometimes called hogs.

Sheep are useful farm animals, too. Sheep are raised mostly for their thick, heavy hair, which we call wool. Each spring the wool is cut, or shorn from the sheep. Then it is sent to factories where warm cloth and clothing are made from it. The meat from sheep is called mutton.

Baby sheep are called lambs. They get milk from their mothers as many baby animals do.

Large herds of sheep are raised on specialized farms, or sheep ranches. On these ranches the herds of sheep are cared for by sheepherders and their dogs. The sheepherders drive their big herds of sheep to pasture, or rangelands, in open country. The herders live in camps made wherever the sheep are.

Some farmers raise rabbits for fur and meat. These animals are kept in pens and are fed with grain, vegetables, fruit, and grass or hay.

Rabbits have many babies. These, like most farm animals, drink their mothers' milk.

Many farms have chickens. Chickens are birds. Male chickens are called roosters. The females are hens. The babies are called chicks.

All chickens have sharp claws on their feet. They use these to scratch for food unless they live on specialized chicken farms. On chicken farms the hens are always kept in cages and are given their food.

Chickens are raised for meat and eggs. Baby chicks hatch from eggs. It takes twenty-one days for a chick to grow and hatch. The young birds are covered with fluffy down at first. But soon the down changes to feathers.

Turkeys, ducks, and geese are raised on farms. Some general farmers have a few. But usually these birds are raised on specialized farms. They are fed grain, and find insects, plants, and grit to eat by themselves.

Dogs are kept on farms as pets. They often help drive cows or sheep to pasture.

Cats are kept as pets, too. But they also help the farmers by killing the mice and rats that eat the farmers' grain.

Each day the farmer cares for his animals. He feeds them, waters them, and gives them clean straw to lie on. He milks the cows night and morning.

Buildings on the Farm

Most farm houses used to be built of wood. They were large, for then families were bigger than most families are now. Many older farm houses are still used. But when new farm houses are built they are quite like new city houses. They are often made of brick or stone. And there is a garage for the farmer's car.

Usually the barn is not far from the house. If the farm is a general farm the barn has a high roof. The space under the roof is a loft. Hay is put into the loft. Then it can be pushed down through holes in the loft floor to feed animals below. Cows, and sometimes horses, are kept on the floor under the loft.

On some farms sheds for sheep and pens for pigs are built onto the barn. But on other farms the sheep sheds and pig pens are separate buildings away from the barn.

Chicken houses are separate buildings. Inside a chicken house there are boxes, or nests, for hens to lay eggs in. There are long poles where hens sleep, or roost, at night.

On specialized chicken farms the chicken houses have rows of cages with just one hen in each. When hens lay eggs in these houses the eggs role down a metal slope to a place where they are gathered and made ready for sale in egg cartons.

If a farmer has cows there is almost always a silo near his barn. A silo is a tall round building with no windows. Silos are used to store cut-up green corn or other plants for feeding cows in winter.

There were no silos until farmers had plant-chopping machines. Now machines chop the green plants quickly, and then the plants are blown through a pipe into the silo.

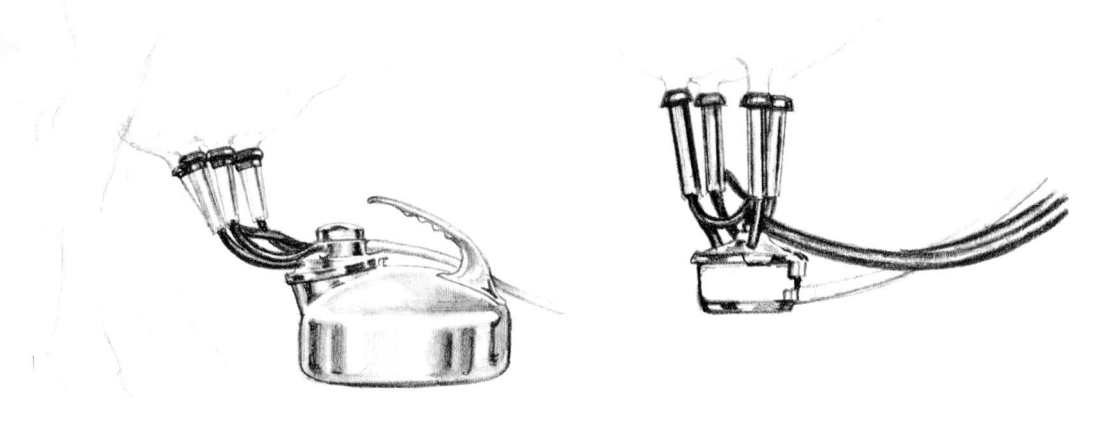

On a farm that has many milk cows there is always a milk house. The milk house is a place for taking care of milk after it has come from the cows.

A farmer with only one or two cows can milk them by hand. But if he has many cows and sells milk he uses milking machines. The machines are fastened to the cows after the cows have been washed and brushed. The machines draw the milk from the cows and it runs into covered buckets. On a specialized dairy farm the milk goes from the milking machines through pipes to tanks in the milk house. Milk is quickly cooled with ice in the milk house. Then it is picked up by milk trucks.

Farmers often have a roofed, three-sided shed for their big machines. The sheds have an open side so the large machines can be moved into them easily. The shed protects these important tools from the weather.

A fruit farm has sheds where fruit is packed in boxes. Vegetable, or truck, farms have sheds for packing, too.

A chicken farm has many long chicken houses. Most farms of every kind have a dog house, for almost every farm has one or more good dogs. If there is no dog house the dogs sleep in the barn, or in the house.

How Does the Farmer's Wife Help on the Farm?

The farmer's wife is a busy person. Like all good mothers she takes care of her family. She sees to it that her children and husband have good food. She keeps them clean. She gets the children off to school. Farm wives take children to dentists, to barber shops, and other places they need to go, just as mothers do in the city.

A farm house is kept clean just as all houses are. It must be swept, dusted, and scrubbed. Now most farm wives have the same tools to work with that city wives have. They have vacuum cleaners, electric washers and dryers, and all the other things that make work easier.

Farm homes of long ago did not have electricity. Then the farm wife worked harder. The stove she cooked on had to have wood burned in it to make heat. She had to scrub clothes on a washboard to get them clean. Each day oil lamps had to be made ready for evening. Now a farm home is much like a city home.

Most farms have home gardens where flowers and vegetables grow. The farmer's wife often helps in taking care of the garden. She uses fresh vegetables from it all summer, and picks the flowers for the family to enjoy. And she may can or freeze vegetables for winter use, too. If there are fruit trees on the farm the farm wife cans or freezes fruit also.

Sometimes the farmer's wife has a few chickens to care for. These are raised for meat and eggs for the family.

Even on small farms there is sometimes more fruit, vegetables, and eggs than the family needs. Then the farmer may build a roadside stand. The farmer's wife is the one who most often takes charge of selling things there.

How Do the Children Help?

In every family each person is important. In city life every child, when not in school, has work to do that helps his family. This is true for farm children, too. All children help with washing dishes, keeping things in order, and going on errands. City children go to the store for their mothers. The older ones help with younger brothers and sisters.

Farm children do not often go to stores alone because the stores are far away from the farm. But they also help care for younger children.

Boys and girls on farms may feed chickens and gather the eggs. They drive cows to pasture. They help pick fruit, and gather vegetables. Sometimes farm children have horses, dogs, cats, or other animals of their own to feed and care for.

Before the time of electricity children on farms had many other tasks to do. They brought in water from wells outside the house. They brought in wood for fires to heat the house and the stove. Sometimes they churned butter. They always picked wild berries and nuts. With no electricity and few machines, life was much harder then than it is now.

How Does the Farm Family Have Fun Together?

Everyone—old and young—needs time for fun. We all need time away from work to do what we like. City people and farm people all take time for fun.

In cities there are libraries and museums, movies, and restaurants. There are parks and playgrounds. All of these are places for fun.

Farmers can drive into cities to enjoy city pleasures. And they can drive to the library in the nearest town. City people can drive into the country to enjoy the fresh air and beauty. Reading, watching TV, and listening to the radio or record player give pleasure in city and country.

Farm families always have good fresh air to breathe. They have plenty of room to play without bothering anyone. They have room for pets and other animals. Many farm families can go swimming and fishing near their farms. In the country there are always places for family picnics.

One big pleasure farm families have is the county fair. A fair is a place where farm families can show off their crops and animals. At the fairs there are places for showing the best of the crops raised by the farmers. Sewing and knitting, canned food, and baked food are things shown by the farm wives. For the children there are balloons, games, rides, hamburgers, ice cream, candy—and lots of fun things.

Prizes are given for the best things shown at fairs. The best animals, fruits, vegetables, flowers, and home-made things win ribbons. Farm families are proud when they take home prize ribbons.

How Does the Farmer Make the Best Use of His Land?

A good farmer makes plans to use his land wisely. He learns about the crops he wants to grow. He studies and reads about the ways of good farming.

The farmer knows that all crops do not do well on the same kind of land. So he plants the kinds of crops his land is best for. The farmer uses rough land for pasture. He makes his best land into fields for crops.

When plants grow they use up plant food in the soil. Some growing crops use more of one kind of plant food than others. If the same crop is planted year after year in the same place the soil becomes poor. Plants cannot grow in poor soil. So the farmers change, or rotate, the crops in their fields. In this way different kinds of plant food in the soil are used. Sometimes farmers do not plant a field. They let it rest, or lie fallow, for a season.

Good farmers also improve the soil by using fertilizer. Fertilizer is plant food. There are many kinds made from chemicals that the farmer can buy. Manure from cattle makes good fertilizer, too. The farmer spreads fertilizer evenly over the land. Then it works into the soil and becomes ready for his crops to use for growing.

How Has Farm Life Changed?

In the days before electricity farm life was different. Then most of the people lived on farms. Now most people live in cities or towns.

Long ago farmers raised almost everything the family needed. They grew their own food. From their animals' hides they got leather for shoes. Women could make cloth from the wool of the sheep for clothes. The wives canned or dried much fruit and vegetables for winter use. They had no refrigerators or freezers. Now, with electricity, farm wives work much as city wives do. They have telephones, and can drive to town in a short time. Farm families these days buy many things they need in towns.

Farm children used to walk long distances to one-room schools. Then all of the children were in one room with one teacher. The teacher taught the different grades by turns. While she worked with one group the others studied.

The school was heated by a stove. Drinking water was in a bucket with a long-handled dipper in it for drinking.

Now farm children ride to school in school buses. The buses take them to schools in towns, or to large modern country schools.

Horses were very important to old-time farmers. They, or mules, pulled the plows and other farm machinery. Horses pulled wagons. They pulled the family anywhere the family needed to go—to town, church, or to visit neighbors. Now farmers have few horses. Most farms have none. The tractor does the work horses used to do. Automobiles and trucks quickly take crops and farm people where they need to go.

Why has farm life changed? There are two main reasons. One is electricity. The other is that many machines have been invented. With electricity everyone's work is easier. Electricity lights buildings, warms them, cooks food, and runs many machines.

The machines work fast and make the farmer's life easier. Farmers used to harvest and work most crops by hand. Now only one farmer with his machines can grow more crops than many farmers used to grow. We have more people in the United States than we had years ago. Even so, because of electricity and machines, we do not need so many farmers to raise all the food we eat.

Index

animals, food for, 17, 19-21, 25, 27, 28, 36, 37, 38, 42; care of, 26, 29, 38; on farms, 30-38

barley, 9
barns, 40
beets, 10
buildings, care of, 27, 29; on a farm, 39-44
bulls, 30
butter, 31, 51

calves, 30
canneries, 25
cats, 38
cattle, food for, 27; uses of, 30-31
cattle ranches, 31; horses on, 32
cheese, 31
chicken houses, 41, 45
chickens, 36, 37, 47
chicks, 36, 37
children, work of, 49-51
colts, 32
combines, 15, 16, 17
corn, 9; cutting of, 17, 27; storing of, 42
cotton, 10; growing of, 22
county fairs, 54-55
cowboys, 32
cows, 30, 40, 42; food for, 27, 42; milking of, 38, 43
crop pickers, 24
crops, 5; watering of, 11-13; spraying of, 14; harvesting of, 15-18; best land for, 56
cultivators, 7, 8
cuttings, 10

dairy farms, 31, 43
disks, 7, 8
ditch diggers, 24
ditches, and watering, 11
dogs, 35, 38; houses for, 45
ducks, 37

eggs, 37, 41, 47, 48
electricity, for pumping water, 12, 13; on farms, 46-47, 51, 58, 61

fall, special tasks in, 28
farm life, changes in, 58-61
farmer, work of, 5, 26-29, 38
farmhouses, 39; of long ago, 46
fertilizer, 57
flowers, raising of, 22, 46
food, for animals, 17, 19-21, 25, 27, 28, 36, 37, 38, 42; for people, 17, 19-21, 25; for plants, 56-57
freezing plants, 21, 25
fruit, 47, 48; harvesting of, 18, 27; kinds of, 20-21; canning and freezing of, 21, 25, 47; packing sheds for, 44
fun, of farm family, 52-55

62

geese, 37
general farms, 5
grain, 9; watering of, 11; harvesting of, 15, 16, 17, 28; storing of, 17; kinds of, 19; uses of, 19, 25
grain seeders, 9, 10
greenhouses, 22
ground, plowing of, 6-8

harrows, 7, 8, 9
harvesting, 15-18, 27, 28
hay, 27, 40
hens, 36, 41
hogs, 33
horses, 40; uses of, 6, 32, 60
hothouses, 22

Indians, and maple syrup, 26
insects, spraying of, 14
irrigation, 11-13

lambs, 34
land, best use of, 56-57
leather, 30, 33, 58

machine pumps, 12, 13
machines, for spraying, 14; for picking fruit and vegetables, 18; on farms, 24, 60-61; care of, 24, 29; for chopping plants, 42; for milking, 43; sheds for, 44; *see also names of machines such as* plow, tractor, cultivator, *etc.*
maple trees, sap from, 26

meat, 30-31, 33, 34, 36, 37, 47
milk, 31; house for, 42, 43
milking, 38, 43
mowers, 24
mules, and plowing, 6
mutton, 34

nurseries, 22

oats, 9
oxen, and plowing, 6

pasture, land for, 56
peanuts, growing of, 22
pens, for pigs, 40
people, food for, 17, 19-21, 25
pigs, food for, 19; uses of, 33; pens for, 40
pinwheels, and windmills, 13
pipes, and watering, 12
planting, 6-10, 26
plants, preparing for, 6-8; spraying of, 14; food for, 56-57
plowing, 6-8
plows, 6-8
pumps, machine, 12, 13

rabbits, 19, 36
rain, and plants, 11
rakes, 24
rice, growing of, 22
roadside stands, 48
roosters, 36
rotation, of plants, 57

63

row crops, 10
row seeders, 10
runners, 10
rye, 9

schools, 59-60
seed, planting of, 9-10
seeders, grain, 9, 10; row, 10
sheds, 40, 44
sheep, uses of, 34; raising of, 35; sheds for, 40
sheep ranches, 35
sheepherders, 35
silos, 42
specialized farms, 5; for fruits and vegetables, 18, 20-21, 44; for flowers and plants, 22-23; for trees, 23; for beef cattle, 31; for milk, 31, 43; for sheep, 35; for chickens, 36, 41, 44; for turkeys, duck, and geese, 37; sheds on, 44
spraying, 14, 26
spring, special tasks in, 26
sprinklers, and watering, 12
strawberries, planting of, 10
streams, and watering, 11, 12
sugar beets, 10

sugar cane, growing of, 22
summer, special tasks in, 27

threshing, 15, 16
tobacco, growing of, 22
tractors, 6, 24
trees, raising of, 23
trees, maple, 26
truck farms, 20-21, 44
trucks, uses of, 24-25
turkeys, 37

veal, 30
vegetables, 10, 46-47, 48; harvesting of, 18, 27; kinds of, 19; canning and freezing of, 21, 25, 47; sheds for, 44

watering, 11-13, 27
well, digging of, 12
wheat, 9
windmills, 13
winter, special tasks in, 29
wives, work of, 46-48, 58
wood, uses of, 23; sawing of, 28
wool, 34, 58
work, of children, 49-51; of farmer, 5, 26-29, 38; of wives, 46-48, 58